T0119244

PLAYS FOR PERFORMANCE

*A series designed for
contemporary production and study
Edited by
Nicholas Rudall and Bernard Sahlins*

EURIPIDES

Iphigenia Among the Taurians

In a New Translation by
Nicholas Rudall

Ivan R. Dee
CHICAGO

Library of Congress Cataloging-in-Publication Data:
Euripides.
    [Iphigenia in Tauris. English]
    Iphigenia among the Taurians / Euripides ; in a new translation by Nicholas Rudall.
        p.   cm. — (Plays for performance)
    ISBN 1-56663-114-9 (cloth : alk. paper). — ISBN 1-56663-113-0 (pbk. : alk. paper)
    1. Iphigenia (Greek mythology)—Drama.   I. Rudall, Nicholas.   II. Title.   III. Series.
PA3975.I8R83   1997
882'.01—dc21   97-14819

INTRODUCTION

by Nicholas Rudall

Euripides wrote *Iphigenia in Aulis* shortly before his death in 406 B.C. and a few months before Athens was defeated by Sparta in the Peloponnesian War. *Iphigenia Among the Taurians* was written about ten years earlier. The chronology of events in the two plays is therefore the reverse of their composition. If the plays are to be performed together, it would seem better to ignore the dates of composition and opt for the natural sequence of the story.

Both plays have as a central theme the horror of human sacrifice. In many ways this pivotal fact has been marginalized by literally centuries of scholarship. Human sacrifice was accepted as a "given" element of the myth, an occasion that afforded the possibility of conflict between Agamemnon and Clytemnestra. Recent scholarship has given this central theme more weight, even allowing that it may represent a vestigial memory of actual sacrifice. (The same argument is now acceptably applied to the story of Abraham and Isaac.) It would be a mistake for any contemporary production to ignore the central horror and relegate the issue to merely the given elements of the myth.

The story of the sacrifice of Iphigenia is not to be found in Homer, but secondary sources suggest that Hesiod told of her rescue by Artemis. In any case, her story is a part of the saga of the Fall of the

3

House of Atreus and a frequent subject of fifth-century drama. The chorus of Old Men in Aeschylus's *Oresteia* sings of her sacrifice at the hands of Agamemnon. In Sophocles' *Electra* her death is Clytemnestra's defense for her treatment of Electra and Orestes—as it is in Euripides' version of the play. All in all, her story forms a vital part of the moral dilemmas posed in many extant (and lost) plays.

What strikes our modern sensibility as particularly strange is the number of *different* versions of the story. We are used to single versions of our myths (Abraham and Isaac). Not so for the Greeks of the ancient world. Roberto Calasso, in his provocative and brilliant book *The Marriage of Cadmus and Harmony,* suggests that the retelling and reshaping of the individual stories was central to the prismatic way the Greeks viewed their religious and cultural myths. In other words, whereas we gravitate toward a single version of a story, finding its truth in its uniqueness, the Greeks believed that "truth" could be found only through multiple prisms. This tendency is especially apparent in the *Iphigenia* plays of Euripides. Not only do the two plays present radically different versions of the events, but their own endings suggest that the gods have yet other alternatives. Unfortunately the endings of both plays are corrupt and irredeemably lost; but this affords a modern production the license to rearrange and invent.

These translations are meant for the stage. As with all other plays in this series, the language is meant to be spoken. Euripides presents a curious challenge to the modern translator. His style is not to be captured by a single tone. Achilles speaks quite differently from Agamemnon, Clytemnestra from Iphigenia. *Iphigenia in Aulis* takes place just

4

before the sacrifice. Clytemnestra and Iphigenia have been summoned by Agamemnon on the pretext of a marriage between Achilles and Iphigenia. Remember that this play was written as the Greek world was finally imploding at the end of the Peloponnesian War. We meet Menelaus and Agamemnon—not the mighty heroes of the Trojan War but two venal and callous contemporary generals. They pay lip service to the honor of the sacrifice. In the end the young and the innocent will die so that the war may go on. And their speech patterns are often rough and contemporary, venal and callous too. Achilles, on the other hand, speaks with the gallantry and even the arrogance and pomposity of a knight in armor.

There is humor in these plays. The old man servant at Aulis is a grumpy and hard-nosed fellow, almost reminiscent of the slaves in comedy. *Iphigenia Among the Taurians* has many situations which if not truly comic nevertheless are intentionally amusing. Both plays are remarkably theatrical. The twists and turns of the plots are filled with suspense. Catastrophe is ever imminent. Ultimately it is survived. But the audience is made to face the unthinkable— murder in the shape of human sacrifice.

CHARACTERS

IPHIGENIA, daughter of Agamemnon and
   Clytemnestra
ORESTES, brother of Iphigenia
PYLADES, friend of Orestes, husband of Electra
THOAS, king of the Taurians
ATHENA, patron goddess of Athens
CHORUS
HERDSMAN
MESSENGER

Iphigenia Among the Taurians

Enter Iphigenia.

IPHIGENIA: This is a story of the House of Atreus. Long ago, Pelops, the son of Tantalus, came, with his swift horses, to the city of Pisa and married Hippodameia, the daughter of Oenomaus. They had a son, Atreus. He, in turn, was the father of Agamemnon and Menelaus. I am Iphigenia, daughter of Agamemnon and Clytemnestra. By the banks of the Euripus, where the winds' wild gusts make the black waters of the eternal river churn and spin in endless eddies of foam, my father killed me, cut my throat upon the altar of Artemis, in the famous valley of Aulis, all for the sake of Helen of Troy. So he thought. There, at Aulis, Lord Agamemnon had massed a fleet of a thousand ships. He longed to win for Greece a glorious crown of victory over Troy, to ease the pain of his brother Menelaus by taking vengeance for the rape of Helen. But the fleet could not sail. The winds were stilled. And he sought an answer in the flames of prophecy. Calchas spoke, "Lord Agamemnon, general of the Greek army, you will not launch your ships from this shore until you have sacrificed your daughter, Iphigenia, to the goddess Artemis. She is the goddess of Light. And you promised her the fairest thing that a year's turning would bring forth. Your wife, Clytemnestra, has borne you a child in your house, and you must make her the victim of the goddess." For my beauty, this reward the prophet gave to me.

   Odysseus conceived the plan. They took me

from my mother. And I went to Aulis, thinking I was to marry Achilles. A foolish dream. They took me by force, raised me above the flames, a sword at my throat. But Artemis put a deer in my place, stole me away, took me through the bright light of ether away from the Greeks to this the land of the Taurians. This is now my home. Thoas is king here, a barbarian lord in a land of barbarians. His name means "swift of foot." He runs with wings for feet. Artemis made me a priestess in her temple. And I make sacrifices to her, for she delights in the rites of her festival. Festival! The name alone speaks of joy. For the rest, I am silent: I fear the goddess. (pause) There is an ancient ritual performed here—whenever any Greek lands on these shores. As priestess I am in charge of the preparatory consecration—that alone. Others do the actual killing—things unspeakable—done in the dark shadows of her secret altar.

In the night I had a strange vision. I speak it now to the light of day. There may be solace in that. In my dream I left this land to live again in Argos. There I saw myself asleep in the safety of my childhood room. Suddenly the ground began to heave and shake. I ran outside, and as I stood there I saw the rooftop fall to the ground. My father's house collapsed upon itself, pillars cracked and tumbled to the earth. But in the settling dust one column remained standing. And from its ornate capital a shock of golden hair began to sprout. It spoke with human voice. I dreamt I was the priestess whose office is to kill all strangers. I sprinkled the creature with holy water and then I wept. This is my interpretation of the dream: Orestes, my brother, is dead. He was the one I marked for death. For the pillars of a house are its man-children and those upon whom I sprinkle holy water, die. It can mean nothing else. I have no friends who could be part of my dream. [Strophius had no child when I "died."]

I must now pour the funeral libations for my dead brother. Though he is far, far away, that is the least I can do. My attendants will help me. They are Greek women whom the king has given to me. They should be here with me. Where are they? In the meantime, I shall go into the chambers where I live, here in the temple of the goddess. *(exit Iphigenia)*

(enter Orestes and Pylades)

ORESTES: Look around. Take care. See if anyone is here.

PYLADES: I shall. Nothing will escape me, Orestes.

ORESTES: Pylades! Is this the temple do you think?— Is this what we came from Greece to find?

PYLADES: I think so. We must have come to the right place.

ORESTES: Is this the altar where Greek blood is spilled?

PYLADES: Look at the surface—it is stained with congealed blood.

ORESTES: Look at that—there on the temple wall!

PYLADES: Offerings to the goddess, yes, trophies taken from the corpses of murdered guests. I will go and look around, take a closer look. *(Pylades enters the temple)*

ORESTES: *(alone)* Apollo! Why? Why have you once more trapped me in the net of your prophecies? I avenged my father's murder. I killed my mother. And I was hunted by wave upon wave of avenging

13

Furies, far from my home, crossing the earth, back and forth, unceasing. I came to you and asked you how I might escape from the rack of madness, from the torture and the suffering that drove me headlong across the land of Greece. You told me to come here, among the Taurians, where your sister Artemis has many altars. You told me to steal a statue of the goddess, an image which men say fell from heaven into this temple. I was to get the statue, by luck or trickery, and then, success in my hands, I was to present it to the land of Greece. That was all you told me. Except that if I did as you commanded, I should have rest from my pain. I listened to your words, O Lord Apollo, and I have come here to this strange, this savage land. *(Pylades returns)* Pylades, what are we to do? You have given me great help in all my labors, what now? The walls are high, impossible to climb. Shall we just go in through the temple entrance? We would be seen, for sure. Perhaps we could force a side entry, crack the bolts. But then if we were caught it would mean certain death. It is impossible. Let us go back, while we can, to the ship that brought us here.

PYLADES: To run away is not acceptable. That is not who we are. We must obey the god. We are not cowards. For the time being, let us leave the temple. We can hide in the cave that is washed by the dark waters of the sea. It is, as we saw, far enough away from our ship. For if someone were to see where it is anchored and told the authorities, we would have no chance. We must wait for night's dark eye. Then we shall make our attempt, use our wits to get the statue from the temple. Look—there is a gap between the walls, there by the carvings on the pediment. We could let

14

ourselves down and get inside. A good man is prepared to face all danger. Cowardice means failure.

ORESTES: You are right. We have not come all this way only to turn back at the last minute. What you said was good. I concur. We will go into hiding, find a safe place. If then the oracle proves false, the blame cannot be laid on me. We must have the courage to act. We are young. We must face the danger. *(they leave)*

(enter Chorus)

CHORUS: Keep holy silence, you who live by the thundering rocks of the savage sea.
Artemis, daughter of Leto, Virgin Huntress of the Hills!
We are here to serve your priestess,
The virgin keeper of the keys.
In this holy procession we come to your sanctuary
Where the pillars hold on high a roof of gold.
We are slaves.
Once we were Greeks
Who lived in her proud towers there in the land of fine horses
Where the fields are green and the woodland rich.
We once were Greeks. Now we are slaves.

(Iphigenia appears)

CHORUS: We have come in haste. Why did you call? What has happened?
Why were you afraid? We have come to the temple,
O daughter of our king, daughter of Agamemnon who sailed to Troy with a thousand ships and ten thousand men.

IPHIGENIA: My friends, I come to you in the midst of deepest lamentations,
Songs of woe sung in a key unloved by the Muses,
In grief for the death of a kinsman. Heavy is the grief that lies upon me.
I mourn for my brother's life. In the darkness of this last night I had a vision,
A dream of darkness. I am finished, finished.
The house of my fathers is no more.
Alas! My family is gone and left no trace.
Fate, you have stolen my brother from me.
You have sent him to the darkness of Hades. My only brother!
I wet the earth for him with these libations, the cup of the dead,
Milk from the cattle in the hills,
Wine from the vine of Dionysus
And honey from the hives of tawny bees.
This is our ancient ritual that soothes the pain of the departed.
Hand me the cup of gold, Hades' offering.
Oh son of Argos, you who are now beneath the earth, we offer these gifts to the dead.
Accept them. I cannot bring a lock of my golden hair to your tomb.
I cannot bring my tears. I live here, far from my home, far from you.
And yet in the mind of the world I lie there with you, dead, cruelly slaughtered.

CHORUS: I will answer you, my sweet mistress, in a song of grief,
A dirge for the dead,
A song touched by the melodies of barbarous Asia,

16

A song sung by Hades himself, a dirge for the
    defeated dead.
"I grieve for the House of Atreus.
The light that danced upon its golden scepter is
    gone.
Gone is the glory of its great palaces. Gone is the
    glitter of its gold.
Gone is the power of kings. Sorrow falls like rain
    upon the house.
The chariot of the sun stopped in the sky and
    wheeled around.
The sacred center of the light of day was driven
    from its course.
The golden lamb brought upon this house pain
    upon pain, woe upon woe, death upon death.
Time out of mind was Tantalus. And retribution
    feeds on the House.
Fate, dipped in evil, will not let you rest."

IPHIGENIA: I have lived a life that was cursed from
    that first moment,
From the night that saw my mother's marriage,
From the night that saw my conception.
From the first the goddesses of Life and Fate
    have conspired against me.
My life has been a hard lesson of pain.
My mother had been won by the noblest of the
    Greeks.
And I was the first fruit of the seed sown in the
    dark chamber of Leda's daughter.
I was born and raised to die, murdered for my
    father's mistake,
Made a victim for my father's arrogance against
    the goddess.
They brought me to the yellow sands of Aulis.
I stood in the chariot, a young bride—ah! the
    mockery of it—

17

A young bride for Achilles, son of Thetis. Ah,
    alas, alas.
Now I live here by the shores of the savage sea, a
    stranger amongst strangers,
Where there is no laughter, no husband, no
    child, no home, no love.
I cannot sing songs to Hera, goddess of Argos.
I cannot weave storied pictures on my singing
    loom,
Pictures of Athena and the Titans! No, I live
    here.
I am a priestess. I steep these altars in a wash of
    blood,
The blood of strangers doomed to death.
And I can hear their screams of pain, and I can
    see the tears they shed.
But even this I can forget. For now I weep for
    the dead in Argos,
For my brother whom I left behind, a babe in
    Argos,
An infant in his mother's arms, a suckling at his
    mother's breast,
There in Argos, my Orestes, my lost prince.

(a Herdsman approaches)

CHORUS: I see a herdsman coming from the shore.
Perhaps he has a message for you.

HERDSMAN: Daughter of Agamemnon and Clytemnestra, I bring you strange news.

IPHIGENIA: Is there some danger? What is the news?

HERDSMAN: Two young men have landed. They
crossed safely through the Rocks of Thunder and
are here. The goddess will be pleased to have a
new sacrifice. There is no time to waste. Make

18

ready the holy water and begin the rites of consecration.

IPHIGENIA: Where did they come from? Can you tell
from the way they are dressed?

HERDSMAN: They are Greeks. That I know and *only*
that.

IPHIGENIA: Did you find out—did someone hear
their names?

HERDSMAN: One called the other Pylades.

IPHIGENIA: And the other's name?

HERDSMAN: Unknown. No one heard it mentioned.

IPHIGENIA: Where did you see them? How were they
captured?

HERDSMAN: Where the waves of the savage sea break
on the—

IPHIGENIA: Why were herdsmen down by the shore?

HERDSMAN: We went there to wash our cattle in the
sea.

IPHIGENIA: Answer my question—Where did you capture them and how? I need to know. The altars of
the goddess have waited long for the red blood of
Greeks.

HERDSMAN: We brought our cattle down from the
woodland to the shore—right opposite the Thundering Rocks. We found a cave there in the cliff,
hollowed out by the constant beating of the
waves. Local fishermen use the spot to collect the
shells that make our purple dye. Anyway, one of
our herdsmen saw the two sitting there. He
stopped and then made his way back to us,
silently, on tiptoe. "Look," he said. "Two gods are

sitting by the shore." One of us—a religious man, devout, you know—raised his hands in the air and began to pray. "Lord Palaemon, guardian of ships, son of the sea goddess Leucothea, look kindly upon us. If the two that sit upon our shore are Castor and Pollux, the favorite sons of Nereus, father of the fifty nymphs—" At this point someone interrupted—a real sinner, doesn't believe in a thing—and he started laughing at the man who was praying. "They're only sailors," he said. "Shipwrecked. They're sitting there by the cave because they're afraid. They must have heard that we make human sacrifices here, kill all strangers." Most of the rest of us agreed with him, and we made up our minds to hunt them down, capture a couple of victims for the goddess. Suddenly one of them left the rock where he was sitting and stood by himself. His head began to shake—violently. He groaned, and a spasm ran through his whole body. He seemed to snap, lose his mind. He began to talk like a hunter, "Pylades, look there, don't you see it? There—the dragon of Hell. She's after me. She is staring me down—and she has vipers for teeth. She is breathing fire, murder, and death out of her very pores. Look, she has left the ground—she hovers above me, my mother in her arms! She has a huge stone in her claws—she is going to throw it at me! Aaagh, she will kill me—where can I run to?"

There was nothing there. Nothing. I think he had heard the dogs barking and the bellowing of the cattle. They say the Furies sound like that. Anyway, we huddled together. Dead still. Waiting. Afraid. He drew his sword and rushed into the herd. He pounced like a lion. He slashed at their sides with his steel blade. He stabbed them in the ribs. I think he fancied he was attacking the Fu-

ries, beating them off him. He continued to attack the cattle until the sea grew flowers of blood.
When we saw our cattle being slaughtered—
hacked to death—each of us picked up a weapon.
We blew on conch shells to summon men from
the surrounding countryside. We did not think
that we herdsmen were powerful enough to over-
come these young, strong newcomers. It didn't
take long for quite a few people to join us. But he
suddenly seemed to lose his fit of madness and
collapsed on the ground, his mouth oozing with
foaming spittle. That was what we needed. As he
fell, we attacked, all of us, pelting him with
stones, rocks, anything. But the other one rushed
to his defense, wiped the foam from his mouth,
cradled him in his arms and protected him from
our stones with his rich, heavy cloak. He just protected his friend, oblivious, loving him, it seemed.
But the first one revived, pushed him aside, saw
this threatening mob surrounding him, and leapt
to his feet. He saw at once that he and his friend
faced an imminent death. He let forth a huge
groan. And we continued hurling stones at them,
moving in closer and closer. The groan became
words of horror and courage. "To our death, Pylades! But death with honor. Draw your sword
and follow me." That was enough for us—those
two sharp swords glinting in those strong hands.
We scattered, back to the hills. But even as we ran
away, some stopped and resumed the attack, pelting them with stone after stone. If they seemed to
be protecting themselves, this gave us heart and
more of us returned from the woods, pelting
them with more and more stones. But it was un-
believable. There was a rain of stones, from
countless hands, yet the victims of the goddess remained untouched. Finally we did get the better

21

of them—thanks more to sheer numbers than individual courage. We hemmed them in, knocked the swords from their hands, and, exhausted, they sank to the ground. We took them to the king. He just looked at them and sent them packing—to you, to the holy waters and the bowls of blood. You should offer a prayer, my priestess, that other strangers, as fine as these, be sent as victims to the altar. A few more carcasses like these and Greece will pay in full for slaughtering you. She will get what she deserves for the sacrifice at Aulis.

CHORUS: You tell a tale of wonder—the madness of this man who has come from Greece across the savage seas. Who can he be?

IPHIGENIA: So be it. Bring the strangers here to me. I will make preparations for the ritual.

(exit Herdsman)

IPHIGENIA: Oh my poor heart—once you were a gentle thing, filled with mercy toward all strangers. You wept for your own people, you broke in pain when Greek men were captured and brought to you. But no more. The dark dreams of night have made me savage: Orestes no longer looks upon the light of day. And so, whoever you are, you will find a heart of steel when you come before me. My friends, I have found a truth, often told but true. Those who have fallen from prosperity feel only envy for those that have it. Why oh why could Zeus not have sent upon his winds, safe through the Rocks that Thunder, some great ship with Menelaus on board, or Helen, she that caused my destruction? Then I would have had my revenge. Then I would have made this place another Aulis where the Greeks trussed me up

like a calf and tried to kill me and my father was
the priest! I cannot wipe that memory away. The
misery lives with me. I reached up to him—oh
how many times!—and wrapped my arms around
his knees and clung to them and said, "Oh my father, think of the shame! To give your daughter
away like this. The Greek women and my mother
are singing marriage hymns. And you cut my
throat. The whole house sings with the sound of
flutes and I am dying. You enticed Achilles here,
the noble son of Peleus. You say he will be my
husband. No, I am the bride of Death. You
brought me here in a golden chariot to this marriage stained with blood. You have betrayed me,
father." They had covered my eyes with a fine veil.
I could not take my little brother in my arms—my
sweet lost brother. Nor did I kiss my sister good-
bye. For I was going to Achilles' palace. And that
is the custom born of modesty. No, I was saving
such expressions of love for later. For I would
soon be back in Argos. So I thought. Oh Orestes,
I grieve for you. You would have been lord over a
great fortune and been king where your father
was king. The goddess has two faces. And I like it
not. If any man stains his hand in bloodshed, if
he touches a woman who is giving birth or lays a
hand on a corpse, the goddess marks him as unclean and keeps him from her altars. But *she,* oh
she delights in the blood of sacrificial murder!
They say Leto is her mother. The wife of Zeus
could not condone such blood lust. As for me, I
do not believe the ancient story, the myth that
says that Tantalus served the gods a meal of
human children. No, it is humanity itself, being
itself a killer, that lays its guilt upon the gods.
That is what I believe. No god could be so evil.
(exit)

CHORUS: Dark, dark are the pathways of the sea
Across the savage deep
Where Io winged her way from Argos,
Crossing from Europe
Into Asia's land.
Who are these men, come from Eurotas,
Thick with green reeds, or from Dirce's holy
streams?
Why have they come to this dark and savage land
Where Artemis drowns her altars in human
blood
And the pillars of her temple drip warm and
red?

Was it gold, more gold,
That dipped the oars and hoisted sails
Across the savage deep?
Hope is a precious gift.
But turned to greed
It takes its toll in grief.
For men will roam with clouded eyes,
Scouring the seas and cities numberless
In search of gold, more gold.
One man wins, one man loses.

How did they slip between the Rocks that
Thunder,
Skirt the Promontory of Stormy Phineus,
Sweep along the Surge of Amphitrite,
Where Nereus's fifty daughters dance and sing?
They raced before the wind that filled their sails
As rudder creaked and prow dipped deep,
As Zephyr's breath brought them to the White
Beach,
The land of many birds, where Achilles once
Raced like a god by the Inhospitable Sea.

I pray that the prayers of my mistress be
    answered.
Come, Helen, Leda's darling daughter,
Come from Troy
With your soft white throat
Ripe for the knife,
Your golden curls matted with blood.
Come to my mistress's arms.
Then the score would be settled. Blood for
    blood.

But I would weep for joy if some Greek
    wanderer
Would come
And put an end to our exile,
An end to our slavery.
I long to go home. I dream of home,
My father's halls and sweet songs in the darkness
Before sleep.

CHORUS: Here they come—the latest victims of the goddess. Their hands are tied. They come in chains. Do not say a word. These men are a harvest offering to the goddess. The herdsman did not lie. The Greeks have come to the temple. Oh holy goddess, accept these sacrifices—if the barbaric custom of these people pleases you, this public ritual of death. But for Greeks it is an act of sin.

IPHIGENIA: So be it. First I must see that all is prepared according to the commands of the goddess. Release the prisoners. They are sacred and must no longer be bound. *(to attendants)* Go into the temple and make ready all that custom demands for the present ritual. *(aside)* Who was your mother, who your father? Who was your sister if you have a sister? She will have no brother now, when these young men are gone. Who knows upon whom such a fate shall fall? The gods move in their own mystery. No one knows the evil that is to come. Sad strangers to this land, where are you from? Oh you have sailed here from far away. And far from home you will remain forever—in death.

ORESTES: Lady—whoever you are—why do you look so sad? Why add your tears to the trouble that lies heavy upon *us*? A condemned man cannot be counted wise if he seeks to blunt the horror of death by lamentation. When death is near and all hope of rescue is gone, why try to excite pity? Where there was one evil, he makes two. He seems like a fool, and he dies just the same. Things must take their course. We can do nothing. You should not grieve for us. We understand. We know the local custom.

IPHIGENIA: Which of you is called Pylades? Tell me that first.

ORESTES: If that is important to you—this man.

IPHIGENIA: Of what Greek country is he a citizen?

ORESTES: Why is it important to you to know this?

IPHIGENIA: Are you brothers—of the same mother?

ORESTES: We are brothers in love. In birth, no.

IPHIGENIA: And what name did your father give *you*?

ORESTES: I might be rightly called The Unlucky One.

IPHIGENIA: That is not what I ask. That is the gods' business.

ORESTES: If I die without a name, no one can curse me and exult in my death.

IPHIGENIA: Why will you not give me your name? Are you so proud?

ORESTES: You can put my body to death, not my name.

IPHIGENIA: Then at least tell me the city of your birth.

ORESTES: Why ask that of a man about to die?

IPHIGENIA: I ask it as a favor—why will you not tell me?

ORESTES: I am from Argos, mighty Argos, and I am proud of it.

IPHIGENIA: Gods of Olympus! Sir, are you really from Argos?

ORESTES: Yes. From Mycenae, great ancient city.

IPHIGENIA: Why did you leave? Were you sent into exile?

ORESTES: In a way I am an exile, both of my own free will and not.

IPHIGENIA: I am pleased to welcome a man from Argos.

ORESTES: You may be pleased. There is no pleasure in it for me.

IPHIGENIA: Would you tell me something I long to know?

ORESTES: In my current circumstances, that is the least I can do.

IPHIGENIA: You have heard of the city of Troy. It is on everyone's lips.

ORESTES: I wish I had not. I wish I had not even heard of it in my dreams.

IPHIGENIA: They say that it is no more, that it has fallen.

ORESTES: That is true. What you have heard is true.

IPHIGENIA: And Helen? Has she returned to the house of Menelaus?

ORESTES: She has, with a curse upon me and someone near to me.

IPHIGENIA: Where is she? She owes me a lingering debt of evil.

ORESTES: Living in Sparta with her husband.

IPHIGENIA: A woman hated by all the Greeks, not me alone.

ORESTES: I, too, have cause to hate her fateful marriage.

IPHIGENIA: Did the Greeks get back home, as we have heard?

ORESTES: You have so many questions—

IPHIGENIA: Just this one favor—before you are to die.

ORESTES: Ask on. If it pleases you, I shall answer.

IPHIGENIA: Calchas—a prophet—did he return from Troy?

ORESTES: He is dead—that was the story in Mycenae.

IPHIGENIA: Oh holy goddess, I give you thanks. And Odysseus?

ORESTES: He has not yet reached home. But rumor has it he's alive.

28

IPHIGENIA: My curse upon him. May he never return to Greece.

ORESTES: Do not curse him—his whole world is in ruins.

IPHIGENIA: And Achilles—is he still alive?

ORESTES: He is dead. His marriage at Aulis did him no good.

IPHIGENIA: A marriage of treachery it was—for those who were there.

ORESTES: Who are you? Your questions show that you know much about Greece.

IPHIGENIA: I am a Greek. When I was but a child I was—abandoned.

ORESTES: That explains your eagerness to know what is happening there.

IPHIGENIA: And what of the general whom they call the Victorious One.

ORESTES: Who? The man I know could not bear that name.

IPHIGENIA: The son of Atreus, King Agamemnon.

ORESTES: I do not know. Ask no more questions.

IPHIGENIA: By the gods, tell me! Sir, one last favor, tell me.

ORESTES: The poor man is dead. And his death has laid another low.

IPHIGENIA: Dead? How did he die? Ah, my heart is broken.

ORESTES: Why do you weep? Had he anything to do with you?

IPHIGENIA: In time past I wept to make him happy.

ORESTES: His death was a thing of horror. He was murdered by his wife.

IPHIGENIA: I feel deep pity for her that killed and he that was killed.

ORESTES: That is enough. Ask nothing more.

IPHIGENIA: Only this. Is the poor man's wife still alive?

ORESTES: She is dead. Her own son—he killed her.

IPHIGENIA: Oh house steeped in damnation! Why? Why did he kill her?

ORESTES: To take vengeance for his father's murder.

IPHIGENIA: Alas! A cruel justice for an act of evil.

ORESTES: But the gods have taken from him the happiness he won.

IPHIGENIA: Did Agamemnon leave behind another child?

ORESTES: Yes. One daughter, Electra.

IPHIGENIA: I see. Do men ever speak of the daughter that was sacrificed?

ORESTES: Never. Except to say that she is dead and gone from this world.

IPHIGENIA: I pity her. I pity the father that killed her.

ORESTES: She was sacrificed to win back an evil woman. But where was the victory?

IPHIGENIA: And Agamemnon's son—does he still live in Argos?

ORESTES: He lives in anguish, nowhere, everywhere.

IPHIGENIA: Then my dreams lied! I bid you farewell. You were nothing.

ORESTES: And the gods lied. We call them wise, but they too lie like fleeting dreams. If the world of men is troubled, so is the world of the gods. One thing alone can bring heavy grief upon a man: when he has trusted in the words of prophecy, and yet through no fault of his own is brought to ruin. There is such a man. He is known to many.

CHORUS: Alas! What can you tell *us*? What of our parents? Are they alive or dead? Can you tell us?

IPHIGENIA: Listen carefully. I have thought of a plan that could help both you and me. If what I propose is agreeable to all concerned, we can be successful. If I save you, would you agree to take a message for me to Argos? Would you take a letter to my friends there? It was written by a man who was captured here. He did not blame me for his death. He took pity on me and recognized that what I did I was forced to do by the goddess. There has been no one who could take my message to Argos. No one could be moved to take the letter to my friends. But you—I can see that you are of noble birth and you know Mycenae and the people there—you can be saved. Accept this offer, this gift of life with honor, in return for a few written words. But you must leave this man behind. The state and the goddess demand a sacrifice.

ORESTES: Your words are pleasing in all respects but one. To sacrifice this man would be a grief to me beyond bearing. I am responsible for him being in this present trouble. He sailed with me out of pity for my own troubles. It would not be right for me to escape, for you to have a favor done for

31

you, and for him to die. Do what I suggest. Give him the letter. He will do as you ask and take it to Argos. Let death come upon me. I could not face the shame of letting a friend suffer at my expense. And this man *is* a friend to me. His life is as my own.

IPHIGENIA: You have a brave heart. You must come from noble stock, a true friend to a friend. May my brother live and be like you. I have a brother, gentlemen, it is only that I cannot see him. I will accept your offer. I will send this man with the letter and you, you must die. Do you so long for death, sir, that you choose this course?

ORESTES: Who will make the sacrifice? Who is it that can take a human life?

IPHIGENIA: It is I, sir. I am the servant of the goddess.

ORESTES: It is a role I do not envy—a terrible thing to have to do.

IPHIGENIA: I am not free to choose. A heavy necessity lies hard upon me.

ORESTES: How can a woman, even with a sword, kill a man?

IPHIGENIA: My office is only to sprinkle the holy water of sacrifice upon your head.

ORESTES: Who then does the killing, if I may ask?

IPHIGENIA: That function belongs to men who are inside the temple.

ORESTES: And when I am dead, in what tomb will I be buried?

IPHIGENIA: There is a sacred pyre within. Your ashes will be scattered from the clifftops.

ORESTES: If only a sister's hands might dress my corpse for burial.

IPHIGENIA: You pray in vain, whoever you are. She lives far away from this barbarous land. If there is comfort in this—know that, since you are a Greek, I will do all that I can for you. I shall set out rich adornments, cleanse your body with golden oil. I shall pour upon your funeral pyre sweet honey perfumed with mountain flowers. It is time. I shall get the letter from the goddess's shrine. Sir, it is not *I* that does this cruelty. *(to attendants)* Guard them. But do not bind them. *(to self)* Perhaps I shall send news to Argos, to him I love most. It is beyond all my hopes. I shall tell him that one whom he thought dead is still alive. He will believe it and find true joy.

CHORUS: I pity you. On you falls the rain of blood and the holy waters of death.

ORESTES: You need not weep for me. I bid you farewell.

CHORUS: But you, young man, you are blessed with great good fortune. You will walk once more upon the land where you were born.

PYLADES: Where is my good fortune when my friend must die.

CHORUS: [These lines should be assigned to individual chorus members.] A sad return to your home. I pity you. I mourn for your misfortune. Which of the two has the better fortune? I do not know what to think. First I weep for you and then grief seizes me.

ORESTES: Pylades, by the gods above, did the same thought strike you?

PYLADES: What do you mean? I do not understand.

ORESTES: Who is this woman? She asked us all about what happened at Troy. She must be a Greek. She asked if the Greeks had returned home. She asked about Calchas—the great prophet—and about Achilles. She knew their names. And she wept for Agamemnon—asked about his wife and children. She must be a Greek. She must be from Argos. She needed to know what had happened there. That must be why she wants to send a letter there.

PYLADES: That is exactly what I was thinking. I have only one doubt. She talked mostly of famous men, of kings and the terrible things that happened to them. Such stuff is the fabric of common gossip the world over. But another thought occurred to me—

ORESTES: What? Tell me, share it with me.

PYLADES: If you die, I cannot face the world with honor. Together we set sail and together we shall die. I would live my life in Argos and all the country round as a coward and a scoundrel. For that is what most people would call me—even though they're scoundrels themselves. They'd think I betrayed you to save my own skin and get home. They'd go so far as to think I killed you myself. They'd think I took advantage of you, planned your murder so that I'd inherit the throne. For it would come to me, I suppose, being your sister's husband. No. I could not face the shame of that. There is no alternative. My last breath will be breathed with you. With you I shall die, and with your body my body shall be burned. I cannot face the thought of shame. I am your friend.

ORESTES: For god's sake hold your peace! I must face my own death. One grief is enough. It does not need another. You talk of shame and the pain of shame. If you were to die because of my troubles, think of the shame I would feel. When the gods treat me like this, it would be a good thing to die. That is how I feel. But you are a happy man. Your house is untouched by the curse of the gods and the sin of the fathers. Mine is cursed. Mine is without god. If you live, you will father sons of my sister whom I gave you to wife. And so my name will live on. My father's name, too, will not die, with your sons for heirs. No, go on your way— live!—rule in my father's house. When you come again to Greece do this for me, I charge you. Raise a monument of stones and set upon it a memorial of me. Let my sister weep deep for me there. Let her cut her hair in mourning for my death. Tell all how I died—cut down by a woman from Greece, slaughtered in holy sacrifice upon the altar. Look after my sister. Do not leave her when you see the desolation of my father's house, the halls empty of friends. Farewell, my friend. I have loved you more than any man. You have been my companion in the hunt, my companion in the home. You have shared so much of my grief, so much of my pain. Apollo is a prophet. But Apollo has deceived me. He planned this— schemed to send me as far away from Greece as possible. He is ashamed of his first prophecies to me. I gave him all of me. I obeyed him. I killed my mother. And now it is my turn to die.

PYLADES: You will be buried with full honors. And I will never betray your sister's bed. I weep for you. And I will love you in death even more than in life. But remember this—you are still alive, oracle or no oracle. You are face to face with the jaws of death. But there is still a chance, a slight chance, that the cruel pendulum of fate will swing the other way.

ORESTES: Hush! The oracles of Apollo cannot help me now. Here is the woman coming from the temple.

IPHIGENIA: *(to attendants)* Go inside and make all things ready for the executioners. Here, strangers, on these folded tablets is my letter. This is what you must do. A man in danger can become quickly changed when that danger is past and he is safe. I have a request. I am afraid that whoever takes these tablets to Argos will think them worthless once he safely leaves this country.

ORESTES: What is your request? What is the difficulty?

IPHIGENIA: I want him to swear an oath that he will take this letter to Argos and my friends.

ORESTES: And you, will you swear an oath on your part?

IPHIGENIA: To do what? Tell me.

ORESTES: That you will ensure that he leaves this barbarian land alive.

IPHIGENIA: That is a just request. How else could he deliver my letter?

ORESTES: It is not you. Will the king allow him to leave?

IPHIGENIA: Yes. I can convince him. In fact I will personally put him on board ship.

ORESTES: Pylades, swear. *(to Iphigenia)* Propose an oath that is sacred to the gods.

IPHIGENIA: "I will deliver this letter to your friends." Swear.

PYLADES: I will deliver this letter to your friends.

IPHIGENIA: And I will see you safe beyond the Rocks that Thunder.

PYLADES: Name the god.

IPHIGENIA: Artemis, in whose house I am priestess.

PYLADES: I call upon Zeus, Lord of Olympus.

IPHIGENIA: And if you break your oath and do me wrong?

PYLADES: May I never reach home. And you, what if you do not save me?

IPHIGENIA: May I never live to set foot in Argos.

PYLADES: Listen, there is one thing more.

IPHIGENIA: The oath can be changed, if that is your wish.

PYLADES: There should be this exception. If the ship founders, if the letter and all else that I possess is lost at sea, and if I alone am saved, let the oath no longer be binding.

IPHIGENIA: Let us do this—the more alternatives, the better hope for success. I will read the contents aloud to you—that way you can remember it and tell my friends. There is safety in that. For if the letter is lost at sea, your safety will ensure the safety of my message.

PYLADES: That is acceptable. Both sides are taken care of. Tell me then, to whom shall I deliver this letter and what shall I say to them?

IPHIGENIA: Take these words to Orestes, son of Agamemnon. "She that was sacrificed at Aulis sends you this letter, Iphigenia, dead Iphigenia to those at Argos, but alive still. . . ."

ORESTES: Where is she? Has she come back from the dead?

IPHIGENIA: You are looking at her. Do not interrupt. "My brother, bring me home to Argos before I die. Take me from this land of barbarians, save me from this murderous priesthood, for here I am a priest that must kill strangers."

ORESTES: Pylades, what am I to say? I am lost.

IPHIGENIA: "Or I shall live to be a curse upon the house, Orestes"—I say the name again. You will remember it?

ORESTES: Oh you gods of Olympus!

IPHIGENIA: Why do you call upon the gods? All this is *my* concern.

ORESTES: Go on. It is nothing. My mind wandered. *(aside)* If I were to ask you, would I find—no, it is past belief.

IPHIGENIA: Then say, "The Goddess Artemis put a deer in my place and saved me from death. My father believed that he was thrusting a sharp blade into my throat. He was not. The goddess spirited me away and brought me to this land."

PYLADES: It is easy to keep your oath, dear lady. It is an excellent oath. It will not take me long to keep my word. *(to Orestes)* Here is a letter. I bring it to you from your sister here.

ORESTES: I give you thanks. But I shall wait to open it. First I take a gift of pleasure that no mere words can give. My sweet sister, my mind swims in awe, in disbelief. Let me hold you in my doubting arms. Let me hold you so my dying soul may dance again.

CHORUS: Stranger! This is not allowed. You are defiling the servant of the goddess. You must not lay hands upon her sacred robes.

ORESTES: O sister, my sister, daughter of Agamemnon, my own father, do not reject me. Here is the brother you never thought to see again.

IPHIGENIA: My brother? Do not mock me. He is in Argos.

ORESTES: Dear girl, he is not there.

IPHIGENIA: And the daughter of Tyndareus the Spartan—Clytemnestra is your mother?

ORESTES: Even so. And my father is the son of Atreus.

IPHIGENIA: How can you prove this to me?

ORESTES: Ask me anything about our father's house and I will answer.

IPHIGENIA: No, you must do the talking. I will be the judge.

ORESTES: I shall tell you first of something Electra told to me. You remember the quarrel between Atreus and Thyestes?

IPHIGENIA: I do. They quarreled over a lamb of gold.

ORESTES: Do you remember embroidering the story on fine cloth?

IPHIGENIA: Oh my dearest brother, your thoughts sing in harmony with mine.

ORESTES: You embroidered an image on the cloth— the sun god turning his face away?

IPHIGENIA: I did indeed create such an image in cloth of gold.

ORESTES: At Aulis, did you receive the holy water sent by your mother for your marriage?

IPHIGENIA: I did indeed. Ah, that glorious marriage which swept me away.

ORESTES: And did you not cut a lock of hair to be taken back to your mother?

IPHIGENIA: I did, to be placed on my empty tomb in memory of me.

ORESTES: I can give you more proof—things I saw with my own eyes. In our father's house we kept an ancient weapon, the spear that Pelops used to kill Oenomaus when he won Hippodameia. We kept it hidden away in your room in the women's quarters.

IPHIGENIA: Oh most loved of all the world. Most loved. Nothing can compare. Orestes! I hold you in my arms, my darling brother. Far from our home in Argos, I hold my loved one in my arms.

ORESTES: And I can hold you close, my sister, whom we thought was dead. I weep. We weep together, tears that flow in streams of sorrow but tears, no less, of rapture and of joy.

IPHIGENIA: When I left you, you were still a babe in arms, cradled by your loving nurse. My heart breaks with happiness. I have no words. Beyond telling, beyond a miracle is this joy that has come upon me.

ORESTES: Now and forever we shall be happy.

IPHIGENIA: Oh my friends, this joy cannot be measured. I am afraid it will take wing and fly from me into the empty air. Oh land of my fathers, Argos, loved Mycenae where the Cyclops lit their fires, I give thanks to you for nurturing my brother, for raising him to be the light of our house.

ORESTES: We were blessed in birth, my sister, but cursed in life.

IPHIGENIA: I remember, oh I remember. I see my father, the knife at my throat.

ORESTES: Although I was far away, I see you too there at the altar.

IPHIGENIA: They did not bring me to a marriage, to the bed of Achilles. No, my brother, they tricked me. At this altar, no joy but tears and lamentation. I weep now for the holy water of death.

ORESTES: And I for the horror of my father's deed.

IPHIGENIA: My life has known no father. Without a father I have lived a life of sorrow. The gods have cursed my life.

ORESTES: And you almost killed your own brother— think on that.

IPHIGENIA: I am a woman most wretched, cursed with a spirit most brazen. I permitted myself to do terrible things, my brother, terrible things. Ah me. I almost killed you, a monstrous murder of my own blood. But how will it end? What will happen now? Is there hope still for a friendly fate? How can I deliver you to safety, send you away from here, away from death and back to Argos? How can I keep the knife from your living blood? Oh my heart, you must do this, you must make it right. Can you leave here on foot, abandon ship? No, death will haunt you as you move amongst savage tribes of men, where no paths can lead to safety. But the sea is savage too, and the Rocks that Thunder dangerous to navigate. What can I do? What god, what man, what blind fate can show us the light of safety? Who will protect us, poor remnants of the House of Atreus?

CHORUS: This is a story stranger than any story ever told. And I have seen it with my own eyes. I shall tell it—with myself for witness.

PYLADES: Orestes. For you to embrace each other in love is both right and natural. But it is time to leave behind your shared grief and joy. For we must escape from this barbaric land. We are on the crest of good luck. We would do well to ride it and win yet more joy.

ORESTES: You are right. If we help it, this good luck can bring us to safety. When men join with them, eager and bold, the gods themselves are more likely to succeed. This I believe.

IPHIGENIA: You cannot stop me now. I must know more. Tell me about Electra. I love her too. What kind of life has she led?

ORESTES: She is happy. She is married to this man.

IPHIGENIA: Where is he from? Who is his father?

ORESTES: From Phocis. Strophius is his father—

IPHIGENIA: —who married the daughter of Atreus. Then he is a blood relation?

ORESTES: Your cousin and my one true friend.

IPHIGENIA: When my father "killed" me, he was not yet born?

ORESTES: No. Strophius had no children for some time.

IPHIGENIA: I greet you, husband of my sister.

ORESTES: And the man who has saved my life.

IPHIGENIA: Let me ask . . . our mother . . . the horror of it . . . how could you do it?

ORESTES: We must not speak of it. I took vengeance for my father.

IPHIGENIA: But why did she kill him, her own husband?

ORESTES: That is for her to know. We must not speak of it.

IPHIGENIA: I say no more. And after his death, did Argos turn to you?

ORESTES: Menelaus is king. I am in exile from my father's land.

IPHIGENIA: When you were brought so low, did he, our uncle, take advantage of you?

ORESTES: No. The Furies and my fear have driven me into exile.

IPHIGENIA: The fit of madness that you suffered on the shore—was that their doing?

ORESTES: Yes. And this was not the first time that men have seen me in their grip.

IPHIGENIA: I understand. The Furies pursue you because of our mother.

ORESTES: Yes. They have put a bit in my mouth to make it bleed.

IPHIGENIA: And why did you come here?

ORESTES: The oracle of Apollo commanded me to.

IPHIGENIA: Why? Can you speak of it, or must it not be spoken?

ORESTES: I can speak of it. This is how my many troubles began. When it was time for my mother to— when it fell upon me to do that evil thing of which we must not speak, I was driven into exile, pursued by the Furies. Apollo sent me first to Athens. There I was to give satisfaction to those goddesses that should not be named. There is a court established there, set up as sacred by Zeus to judge Ares for some act of pollution. I went to Athens. At first no one would touch me, as I too was polluted, hated by the gods. Some men took pity on me and took me in. But though we shared the same roof, I sat apart, alone. They would not speak to me. I shared their food and drink, but in silence, apart, alone. They served the wine not in a common bowl but in separate cups. Each man had his equal measure, and so they took their pleasure. I knew it was not right to question my hosts, so I kept silent and I grieved alone. I pretended not to notice. But deep inside I was torn with grief, for I was the murderer of my mother. This was what we did. And my misfortunes have now become a sacred ritual in Athens. They drink in silence at the Feast of Cups. And then I came

44

to the hill of Ares, the Areopagus. I stood trial. I was the defendant. The oldest of the Furies stood as prosecutor. Arguments were presented about my mother's death. Apollo himself intervened. His testimony saved me. The jury of twelve men voted six to six. Athena cast the deciding vote, and I was acquitted. Some of the Furies agreed with the verdict and took a place of sanctuary there by the court itself. Some did not. And they pursued me, hounded me, a homeless wanderer across the earth. I went again to Apollo's sacred shrine. There I threw myself upon the ground. I took no food. I swore I would kill myself upon the rocks below if Apollo who had brought me to ruin refused to save my life. Apollo spoke. Words came from the golden tripod, and I was sent here. My mission is to seize the statue of the goddess, the image that fell from the sky, and take it back to Athens.

If you can help me do this, I will be saved. If we can carry off the statue of the goddess, I will be cured of my madness and take you with me aboard our sleek ship and we will go home again, home to Argos.

Oh my sister, whom I love above all the world, save our father's house, save your brother. We are as nothing, and the House of Atreus is as nothing if we do not carry off the idol that fell from the sky.

CHORUS: Still we see before us the anger of the gods. Still it seethes, strange, terrible. Still it drives the seed of Tantalus through paths of woe.

IPHIGENIA: Even before you came, my brother, I longed to be in Argos, longed to see your face. I share your desires. I want to set you free from all your pain, to restore you to our father's house,

45

now so afflicted. I bear no ill will toward my father, though in his mind he killed me. That is my desire—to save our house and keep my hands clean of your blood. But I fear the goddess. Her eyes see everything. I fear the king when he finds the marble pedestal empty, the statue gone. I shall be put to death. There is nothing I can say in my defense. But if we can find success in both your plans—to carry off the statue and take me with you on your ship—then all danger is worth facing.

If you take the statue and I am left behind, I will surely die. But you will be free and win a safe return to Argos. I am prepared. I will face death to save you. In my mind there is no doubt. The death of a man lies heavy upon his house; a woman's life is of little worth.

ORESTES: Do not talk like that. I will not be your murderer as well as my mother's. Our hearts are one. We must live as one—or die as one. If I can escape, I shall take you with me. If not, we shall face death together. I have been thinking. If Artemis opposed this plan, how could Apollo, her brother, have commanded me to take the statue to Athens? Why would he have allowed me to see your face again? No, when I think on this I have strong hopes that I will get home again.

IPHIGENIA: But how can we do it? We might escape, but how could we bring the statue with us? That is what makes it so impossible, long for it as we may.

ORESTES: We might be able to kill the king.

IPHIGENIA: No. It is an abomination to break the law of guest friendship.

ORESTES: But if it would save us we must do it.

IPHIGENIA: I could not do it. But I stand in awe of your boldness.

ORESTES: What if you were to hide me in the temple?

IPHIGENIA: And then in cover of darkness you would remove the statue?

ORESTES: Yes. Night belongs to thieves. Daylight shines on honest men.

IPHIGENIA: There are guards within the sacred precinct. We could not get by them.

ORESTES: There is no hope then. We cannot escape.

IPHIGENIA: I have an idea, a complicated plan.

ORESTES: Tell me. Share it with me.

IPHIGENIA: I can make use of your present misfortune.

ORESTES: How? Your woman's mind is too clever for me.

IPHIGENIA: I shall say you have killed your mother, that you are a matricide from Argos.

ORESTES: Make use of my misfortunes if they can help.

IPHIGENIA: I shall say that it is forbidden to offer you to the goddess.

ORESTES: On what grounds? Though I begin to see.

IPHIGENIA: Because you are polluted. I may only make sacrifice of that which is pure.

ORESTES: And how will this help us get our hands on the statue?

IPHIGENIA: I will say that you must be made pure, washed clean in the waters of the sea.

ORESTES: But the statue—the reason why we came here—will still be left in the temple.

IPHIGENIA: I shall say that you touched it and it is defiled. It too must be washed clean.

ORESTES: Where will you perform the purification? In some harbor or inlet of the sea?

IPHIGENIA: Where your ship is anchored and moored with ropes to the shore.

ORESTES: Will you or someone else carry the statue?

IPHIGENIA: I will. I alone am permitted to touch it.

PYLADES: And Pylades? What shall he do?

IPHIGENIA: I shall say that he too is defiled.

ORESTES: Will you do this in secret or will you tell the king?

IPHIGENIA: I shall tell him. He will believe my story. It could not be done without his knowledge.

ORESTES: The oarsmen on the ship must be at the ready.

IPHIGENIA: That is for you to make sure of.

ORESTES: There is one thing more. These women must keep this a secret: you must persuade them. Beg them. Use your power as a woman to awaken their pity. For the rest, I have hope and confidence in success.

IPHIGENIA: *(to Chorus)* My dear friends, I am counting on you. Into your hands I place my future life. Either I will find happiness or become as nothing, no home, no dear brother, no sweet sister. Let me ask you to remember this most of all. We are women, we find comfort in this sex we share, we must trust each other, protect our common interests.

Keep our secrets safe. Help us. Help us escape. Your silence will win you respect. Look at us. See three dear friends caught in one snare: we die or we make a safe return home.

If I am saved, I will not forget you. I will, in turn, save you and bring you back to Greece. I beg of you, I take you by the hand—and you, I touch your cheeks. I fall before you on bended knee. Remember those you love at home. Remember your fathers, your mothers. Remember your children—those that have them. Answer me. Who says yes? Who says no? Speak to me. Will you do it? If my words fall upon deaf ears, I am lost, I and my poor brother.

CHORUS: Courage, my mistress, courage. Save yourself. Great Zeus be my witness, your secret will be safe with us.

IPHIGENIA: Bless you. May you live a happy life. *(to Orestes and Pylades)* Now, go inside the temple. The king will be here soon. He will want to know if the sacrifice has been performed.

(she prays to Artemis) Holy goddess, you saved me once in the groves of Aulis, saved me from a father's murdering hand. Save me now once more. And save these young men. If not, no more will mortal men believe Apollo's words. Be gracious unto us. Grant us leave to flee this savage land and go to Athens. This land is not where you belong. Let us take you to the holy city that awaits you.

CHORUS: Halcyon! Sad bird of the reefs of the sea,

49

Your shrill lament touches the heart.
You mourn for your mate lost forever,
For your lonely life.
I am a wingless bird, and my sad heart
Sings its echo of your laments.
I long for my home, the crowds in the streets,
Long for the temple of Artemis, goddess of
    mothers,
There where the palm fronds sway in the breeze
And the laurel shades the green shoots of the
    olive,
Where Leto gave birth by the spinning circle of
    waters
And the swans sing their homage to the Muses.

My tears scarred my cheeks, ran like rivers of
    pain
That day, oh that day, when my city fell
And I was dragged to the ships,
A slave sold for gold,
Savaged by the spears of barbarians.

Here I serve the daughter of Agamemnon,
Priestess of Artemis.
We are the killers of Greeks.

The man who knows no happiness
I envy.
For pain is his friend, and he knows nothing but
    pain.
But when misery replaces joy,
When tears flow where there was laughter,
Being human is a grief too heavy to bear.

Iphigenia, you will embark on a ship of fifty oars.
You will find your home again.
The pipes will breathe spirit into the oarsmen.
Apollo will sing you home, his lyre stirring
The waters where Athens gleams its welcome.

I will be left behind as the oars dip
And the sails swell over the prow
And the ship speeds into the deep.

If only I could fly like the sun
Where the air is a fine fire,
And beat my wings over my own rooftops.

Oh to dance free again!
Where once I whirled in the wedding dance
Surrounded by friends, veils all aglitter,
My ebony hair curled on my white cheeks.
Oh to dance free again!

THOAS: Where is the Greek woman who is priestess
of this temple? Has she begun the rituals for the
captive strangers? Is the sacrifice complete? Are
their bodies now burning on the bright flames of
the funeral pyre?

CHORUS: Here she is, my lord. She can tell you herself.

(enter Iphigenia, with statue)

THOAS: Daughter of Agamemnon, why are you carrying the statue of the goddess? Why did you take it
down from its sacred pedestal?

IPHIGENIA: Stay where you are, my lord. Do not come
near.

THOAS: What is it, Iphigenia? Is there something
wrong within the temple?

IPHIGENIA: Wash it clean! All must be pure!

THOAS: Why do you say this? Tell me.

IPHIGENIA: The offerings you hunted down for me
were unclean, my king.

51

THOAS: Do you know this for certain? Or do you just suspect it?

IPHIGENIA: The statue of the goddess turned its face from us.

THOAS: Was there some shaking of the earth or did it move by itself?

IPHIGENIA: It moved by itself. And it closed its eyes.

THOAS: What could be the cause? You say the strangers are unclean?

IPHIGENIA: That alone is the cause. They have committed a terrible crime.

THOAS: Did they kill some of our people down by the shore?

IPHIGENIA: No. Blood was on their hands when they arrived, the blood of their own kin.

THOAS: Tell me more. I want to know.

IPHIGENIA: They killed their mother, together, killed her with a sword.

THOAS: Apollo. We, whom they call barbarians, would not have been so cruel.

IPHIGENIA: They were hunted down, driven out of Greece.

THOAS: And that is why you are carrying the statue outdoors?

IPHIGENIA: Yes, to hold it here beneath the holy sky, to remove the taint of murder.

THOAS: How did you learn that the strangers were unclean?

IPHIGENIA: When the statue turned her face away, I questioned them.

THOAS: That was clever of you to connect the two events. Greece raised a clever child.

IPHIGENIA: That is not all. They tried to seduce my broken heart.

THOAS: Did they try to win you over with some pleasing news from Greece?

IPHIGENIA: They told me that my only brother, Orestes, was alive and happy.

THOAS: They thought you would spare them if they brought good news?

IPHIGENIA: They told me that my father too was happy and well.

THOAS: And you? You remained faithful to the goddess?

IPHIGENIA: Yes. I hate all Greeks. Greece destroyed me.

THOAS: Now tell me, what are we to do with the strangers?

IPHIGENIA: We must follow the law, obey the sacred commands of the goddess.

THOAS: And are the holy waters ready? Is the knife prepared for death?

IPHIGENIA: First the victims must be made clean.

THOAS: In the waters of a spring or in the sea?

IPHIGENIA: The sea washes clean all the sins of men.

THOAS: They will be more pure for the sacrifice.

IPHIGENIA: And my plans will more likely succeed. *(she starts to leave)*

THOAS: Wait. Why not wash them here where the sea breaks against the temple walls?

IPHIGENIA: I need a secluded spot. There is much that I must do.

THOAS: Take them where you wish. I do not want to observe the ritual.

IPHIGENIA: The statue too must be purified.

THOAS: Yes, if the taint of matricide has touched it.

IPHIGENIA: That is why I took it from the sacred spot.

THOAS: That shows your prudence and your piety.

IPHIGENIA: You must do something for me.

THOAS: Tell me.

IPHIGENIA: Put the strangers in chains.

THOAS: How could they escape?

IPHIGENIA: You cannot trust a Greek.

THOAS: Servants! Put them in chains.

IPHIGENIA: Let them bring the men outside.

THOAS: Whatever you wish.

IPHIGENIA: They must cover their heads with their robes.

THOAS: The sun should not see their pollution.

IPHIGENIA: Give me some of your men.

THOAS: They are yours.

IPHIGENIA: And send someone to the city.

54

THOAS: Why?

IPHIGENIA: To warn everyone to stay indoors.

THOAS: To avoid contact with their pollution?

IPHIGENIA: To see them is to be cursed.

THOAS: Go and make the proclamation.

IPHIGENIA: —that no one shall lay eyes on them.

THOAS: You take good care of the city.

IPHIGENIA: Yes, and of my friends to whom I owe so much.

THOAS: Thank you. The city is right to admire you so much.

IPHIGENIA: You must remain here and serve the goddess.

THOAS: How?

IPHIGENIA: Her temple halls are to be cleansed by the fire of torches.

THOAS: So that it will be purified when you return.

IPHIGENIA: When the strangers come out of the temple you must—

THOAS: What am I to do?

IPHIGENIA: Cover your eyes with your cloak.

THOAS: So that I too will have no contact with their pollution?

IPHIGENIA: And if I seem to be taking too long a time—

THOAS: How long should I cover my eyes?

IPHIGENIA: Do not be surprised if it is a long time.

THOAS: Do what the goddess requires. It must be done right. Take your time.

IPHIGENIA: I pray that this purification turns out according to my desires.

THOAS: I share your prayer.

(Orestes and Pylades appear)

IPHIGENIA: The strangers are leaving the temple. I see the robes of the goddess and the newborn lambs whose sacrifice will wash away the stain of murder. I see the torches and all the things I need for the strangers and the goddess. *(she joins the procession)*

I warn all the citizens to keep away. Keep away from this pollution, all you acolytes who serve the god with pure hands, all you who are about to enter upon marriage, and all you who are heavy with child! Keep away! Stand aside! Beware of this pollution!

O virgin queen, daughter of Zeus, if I wash clean the blood guilt of these men, if I reach the place where the sacrifice should be made, you will live in a house that is pure and we shall be happy.

For the rest I keep silent.
The gods know my mind.
For the gods are great.
And Artemis, my goddess, is great.

CHORUS: Beautiful was the god child Apollo
   When Leto bore him in the green valley of
      Delos.
   A golden god she bore, skilled in the harp,
   Whose sister Artemis loves the hunter's bow.
   His mother carried him from that rock by the sea

And brought him to Parnassus, mother of
    rushing waters.
Parnassus where Lord Dionysus holds his revels.
There in the dangerous dark of Hell's oracle,
The scarlet dragon lurked in the bay tree's
    shadow
With black mottled skin and scales of bronze.
This monster of the earth you slew, though yet a
    god child,
Slew the Python and the oracle was yours.
Now you sit by the golden tripod
On the throne of truth.
And from earth's dark depths you give
The light of prophecy to humankind.
By Castalia's holy waters you grace
Your temple at the center of the earth.

But the goddess who kept the truth time out of
    mind,
Themis, she who lived beneath the earth,
Now was dispossessed.
She who had brought the phantoms of the night,
Dreams which told to mortal men as they lay
    sleeping
In the darkness of their beds
Things that had been,
Things that would come.
Thus did Earth, jealous of her daughter's honor,
Rob Apollo of his oracle.
The god child then to Olympus sped
And twined his infant fingers round the throne
    of Zeus
And begged the Father to take back the oracle
From the fury of the Earth.
Zeus smiled to see the god child claim
So rich a prize and nodded his assent.

No more would mortals hear the voices of the
  night,
No more for them the truth revealed in
  darkness.
Apollo reigned once more. And mortals flocked
To hear the god's words bathed in light.

(enter a Messenger who shouts at the temple doors)

MESSENGER: Guards! Attendants of the altar, where is
Thoas, our king? Open the temple doors and call
our king outside.

CHORUS: What is your news, if I may ask?

MESSENGER: The daughter of Agamemnon has
tricked us. The two young men have escaped!
They have fled this land. They have taken our sacred image on board their ship.

CHORUS: I cannot believe your story. But the man
you seek, the king, has just now left the temple.

MESSENGER: Where did he go? We must tell him what
has happened.

CHORUS: I do not know. But go, hurry, and when
you find him, tell him.

MESSENGER: I do not trust you. You women must be a
part of this.

CHORUS: You are out of your mind. We have nothing
to do with the strangers' escape. Go, hurry to the
palace gates.

MESSENGER: No. I have an appointment here first—
with this. *(he seizes the door knocker)* It will tell me
the truth. I will find out if the king is inside.
(knocks) You there, you inside, unlock the bars.
Tell the king that I am here at the gates. I have
terrible news.

58

(Thoas enters)

THOAS: What is all this noise? This is the house of the goddess! Who hammers at the doors and causes such confusion inside?

MESSENGER: Ah! Those women told me you had left. They tried to trick me. But you were inside all the time.

THOAS: Why would they do that? What could they gain?

MESSENGER: Leave them for now. I have important news. The young woman, the priestess here, Iphigenia, has left the country. She took off and took the sacred image with her. The purification nonsense was only a trick.

THOAS: So. That was what it was all about.

MESSENGER: She did it to save Orestes. That's some surprise for you, isn't it?

THOAS: Orestes? The son of Agamemnon?

MESSENGER: He was one of the strangers we were going to sacrifice to Artemis.

THOAS: A miracle sent by the god. It is nothing less.

MESSENGER: Forget that and listen to me. We must devise a plan to chase them and capture them. Listen to me.

THOAS: Speak. I will listen to your advice. They have far to sail before they can escape my power.

MESSENGER: This is what has happened. We had joined the procession, carrying the chains to bind them as you ordered. We arrived at the shoreline where Orestes' ship lay hidden at anchor. Iphigenia signaled us to stand back. She was about to perform the ritual cleansing with fire and the waters of the sea. She took the chains and walked behind the two men, alone. This was suspicious, of course. But we were following your orders. After a little while she let forth a solemn cry. She chanted some unintelligible incantation—part of her magic ritual of washing away the stain of murder. This was to make us think that we were witnessing some important secret ceremony.

We had been sitting there, some distance away, when it occurred to some of us that the strangers —who were now free of chains—might kill her and run away. On the other hand, we did not want to get too close in case we saw something forbidden. So we sat in silence. In the end, though, we all had the same idea at once, and we approached even though it was forbidden. And then we saw it. There was a Greek ship, with its oars splayed like wings and fifty oarsmen poised, ready to row. The young men—no chains on, of course—were standing by the stern. Some crewmen were keeping the ship steady by thrusting long poles into the sand. The anchor was being raised to the catheads. And some men were scurrying to let a rope ladder down from the stern for the strangers to get on board.

We now could see we had been tricked. Ritual be damned! We grabbed the woman and we tried to pull the rudder from the stern of the huge ship. We exchanged words. "Who do you think you are, coming here like pirates, stealing our priestess and our holy statue? Who are you? What's your father's name? Who are you to kidnap our priestess?" He answered, "I am Orestes, son of Agamemnon. This woman is my sister. Yes, I have captured her, and I will take her to the home from which she herself was taken!"

We held on to the woman, held her tight and tried to bring her back here to you. That was when I got these terrible blows to the face. They had no weapons, nor did we. They pounded us with their fists. They kicked us in the stomach and the ribs. They hit us so hard that we had no strength left. And they kept on raining huge heavy blows upon us until all we could do was run to the clifftops, bloody wounds on our heads, our eyes half-closed and swollen. On the cliff we were able to take a stand and begin our own offensive, hurling rocks down upon them. But there were archers on board. And with a hail of arrows they drove us back yet again. Suddenly a huge wave drove the ship close to the beach. The woman could have got on board but she was afraid of the surf. Orestes lifted her on his shoulders and stepped into the sea. He clambered up the ladder and put her safely on board. But not alone. The statue of Zeus's virgin daughter was also placed on board.

From the center of the ship a great cry was raised: "Men of Greece, take your oars, churn the sea until it foams and swirls beneath our ship. We have it! We have that for which we braved the Rocks that Thunder and the savage sea."

They all let out a roar of joy and slashed the sea with their oars. In the safety of the harbor the ship sailed smooth, but when she met the open sea huge breakers smashed against her prow and she began to stall. A sudden squall pushed her backward, stern first. The men struggled hard, but the breakers were too strong. The undercurrent caught her and drove her back toward the shore. Then Agamemnon's daughter stepped forward and offered a prayer. "Queen Artemis, save me, your priestess. Take me from this savage land, home to Greece. Forgive me for stealing your image, goddess. You love your brother, Lord Apollo. Know that I too love my brother Orestes."

The sailors took up a chant, a hymn of praise in response to her prayer. And they began to row, arms bare and glistening. They rowed in unison to the rhythm of command. But the ship drifted nearer and nearer the rocks. Some of us waded out into the water, others made loops of rope to try to fasten the ship to the land. At this point I left. I ran straight here to tell you, my king, what is happening down by the shore.

Bring ropes and chains. If you hurry and the sea does not become calm, we can capture them. Lord God Poseidon, King of the Sea, hates the House of Atreus. He took Troy's side in the war. He will deliver the son of Agamemnon into your hands and the hands of your citizens. Of this I have no doubt. And you will capture his sister who has betrayed the goddess who saved her life at Aulis.

CHORUS: Oh Iphigenia, hapless creature, you will yet again face death. You and your brother. Yet again you have fallen into the hands of the powerful.

THOAS: Call all the citizens! Mount your horses and race to the shore. Seize the ship as she founders. Call upon the goddess to help you capture these unholy creatures. Launch the fleet. With cavalry on land and ships at sea we shall capture them. We shall hurl them from the cliffs or impale their bodies on sharp stakes.

You women, you participated in this. And you will be punished at our leisure. But now we have urgent business to attend to. Let us be gone!

(enter Athena)

ATHENA: King Thoas, where are you taking your men? Listen to me. I am the goddess Athena. Call off your men! Give up the chase! Orestes was sent here by the oracles of Apollo. He was commanded to bring his sister and the sacred image back to my city of Athens. Only then could he escape the anger of the Furies. Only then could he be freed from all his troubles. I give you my word that this is true. You mean to capture Orestes in the stormy waves and kill him. But Poseidon, out of love for me, is now bringing a gentle calm to the rough sea. The ship may sail.

And you, Orestes, hear my voice though you are not near. Hear the voice of the goddess and do what I command. Leave these shores with your sister and the sacred image. When you come to Athens, city built by the gods, you will seek a place on the farthest outskirts, near the rock of Carystus. It is a holy place, and my people call it Halas. Build a temple there and set up the image on a shrine. It shall be called the Shrine of Artemis of the Taurians. It will be an eternal memorial of the agony of your endless journeys pursued by the Furies. At Taurus you were freed, and future generations shall sing hymns to Artemis of the Taurians.

And let this custom be established. Whenever men hold a festival at the shrine, remembering that your life was spared at the altar, let the priest put the knife to the throat of some man. Let him, in the sanctity of the ritual, draw blood. Let Artemis be thus honored.

You, Iphigenia, when you return to Greece, must go to Brauron. There you will be the guardian of the keys of the Shrine of Artemis. At Brauron you will die and be buried there. And each year, in honor of women who die in childbirth, an offering of finespun cloth will be sacrificed and given in your honor.

These women, whose only sin is loyalty, must be sent forth from these shores to their homeland of Greece.

[There is a gap in the text here.]

Orestes, I saved you once before on the Areopagus. There the ballots were equal. And this custom shall live forever: whoever receives equal votes shall be acquitted. Son of Agamemnon, take your sister now. And leave this land.

King Thoas, I speak to you, do not be angry.

THOAS: Queen Athena, if a man hears a god speak and does not obey, he is a fool. I am not angry, neither with Orestes for stealing the image of the goddess, nor with his sister. There is no profit in fighting with the gods and all their power. Let them go to your city. Let them take the statue and with good fortune on their side set it up for worship. As you command, I shall set these women free. They can go home again to Greece. I call off my armed men. I call off my ships. Such is your pleasure, goddess. The strangers are free.

ATHENA: I commend you. Necessity is a mighty force, stronger than you, stronger than the gods. Blow, wind, blow, send the son of Agamemnon with all speed to Athens. I shall accompany them on their journey. I shall protect the sacred image of my sister.

(exit Athena)

CHORUS: Speed on, children of Agamemnon, rejoice in your good fortune. Rejoice in your deliverance. Goddess Athena, among the immortals you are held in reverence by mortal men. We shall do

as you command. I lived without hope. And now great joy has fallen upon me as I heard your words.

Victory! Holy and loved, Victory!

Guide me through this life.

Ever crown me with your glory.